Oh, that I had Wings like a Dove

Touching the Life of a Child

by Denise L. Folks, Ph.D.

DORRANCE
PUBLISHING CO
EST. 1920
PITTSBURGH, PENNSYLVANIA 15238

Dorrance Publishing Co
585 Alpha Drive
Pittsburgh, PA 15238
Visit our website at www.dorrancebookstore.com

ISBN: 978-1-4809-8601-5
eISBN: 978-1-4809-8583-4

"Oh, that I had wings like a dove!
I would fly away and be at rest;
Truly, I would flee far away;
I would lodge in the wilderness,
I would hurry to find a shelter for myself
from the raging wind and tempest."

Psalms 55:6-8

Contents

Dedication ix

Acknowledgments x

Forward xi

I Must 1

Introduction 2

Psalms 55:1-8 5

Wings Like a Dove 6

Defense Fund 7

The Fruit of the Womb 8

A Peace 9

Don't Say That 11

Children Live What They Learn 12

Dear Lord 13

Quote 14

Quote 15

Daddy 16

Help Me, Mommy 17

Encouragement 18

Quote 19

Did You Tell Them? 20

Scripture 21

If All the Children 22

Children's Defense Fund .23

I Ain't Trying to Grow Up 24

Take the Lead 26

Post Partum Disgrace 27

Scripture 29

Dear God 30

Can We Do This Every Day, Dad? 31

Every Day in America 32

Like Sunday Morning 33

Quote 34

I am My Parent's Child 35

Scripture 37

What Did I Do? 38

Inside Job 39

Mistakes 41

Scripture 42

Parents 43

Quote 44

Dear God 45

I Can Handle It 46

Scripture 48

Time to Reflect 49

Little, Little Children .50

The Cortisol Effect 51

Midnight Child 53

Hope 55

Trust 56

Scripture 57

Dear Mommy 58

Quote 61

Dance with Me 62

I Wish I Was Never Born 63

National Statistics 65

Dying to Know 66

Quote 68

Man, that's My Daughter 69

Human Trafficking 71

Quote 72

Quote 73

Quote 74

Getting to Know Malik 75

Scripture 77

Misunderstood in the Hood .78
Beads, Braids, & Barbie Dolls 79
Stifling the Child Within .81
Once Upon a Time 83
Adverse Childhood Experiences 85
Quote 87
I Am 88
Scripture 89
Evolution of Abuse 90
It's the Law 91
Hats Off 92
Generations 94
The Family that Prays 95
A Call to Repent 98
Scripture 99

Dedication

Listen All You Parents

Listen all you parents; Listen with an attentive ear
The children want to talk to you without feeling any fear

I don't like it when you drink, curse, fight, and scream
Or, when you tell me I'm nothing, and shatter my hope, my dream

The clothes that you be wearing, they show all your skin
You make me feel embarrassed. The Bible calls that sin

When I got my period, I thought I was about to die
You yelled at me and shook you head; why would you make me cry?

As I started growing up and really filling out, you criticized me often
You called me fat and stout

Can you be a parent and not my best, best friend?
I need instruction from you, Dad, to go from "Boyz to Men"

Listen all you parents; Listen with an attentive ear
The children want to talk to you without feeling any fear

Acknowledgments

I thank God for calling me to minister to and stand in the gap for children, youth, and families.

I thank children, youth, and families for allowing me to encourage and empower them to seek excellence in body, soul, and spirit.

Foreword

"How could someone who seemed to love me, give me everything I need be so cruel with her words?"

I spent most of my life asking God that question. My mother, a single parent, gave us every material thing that we needed. She was the best mother in the world, as far as we were concerned, until she got angry. When she was upset, for any reason, the poison came out of her mouth: "You are the worst thing I have ever done." "You are no use to me." "Why don't you just lie in the road so a truck could run over you?" "Why did I ever make you?"

These were some of the poisonous words that she spewed. I thought that if this was how my mother; the woman who brought me into the world felt, then no one could ever love me! "I'm really worth nothing." Whatever I did to bring those words out of her was nothing to be compared to the rebellion those words brought out of me. With nothing to lose, I set out on a path of self-destruction; I ran away from home, lied, and messed up homes, with no remorse for anything. I was angry at the world and hated people. It gave me pleasure to inflict emotional pain on other people.

Then, one day, God rescued me from myself. After giving my life to Christ, I still couldn't believe that I was worth loving and continued living with low self-esteem for years until God surrounded me with godly women. They saw that I was "going through." God used them and His word to bring "me out." Now I see myself the way God sees me.

In my walk with God, He taught me about "curses." He revealed to me that I was walking under several different curses. One of the major curses was the one my mother had spoken over my life, all my life:

"you're worth nothing and you'll never be anything." Since my mother wasn't in a place to receive the word of repentance from God, I was responsible to now repent on her behalf even for the sins of her parents before her (up to the fourth generation).

Then God released me to walk in victory and in peace. I wasn't angry anymore. The bitterness started seeping away. I am now emotionally sound and have risen up with fresh strength and ambition, and I don't need validation from anyone but God to be myself and to succeed. Now I'm in the process of starting my own business.

I am calling on all parents to be careful of the poison you spew at your children. You could curse their future. Those of you who have already cursed them, you can now repent, offer them to God and begin to bless their lives by speaking blessings. Don't look at what they are now. Look at what they will become through Jesus Christ.

You children, who have been trying to prosper while under the curse of your parents, let them know you forgive them and release yourself to walk in the blessings of God whose child you now are.

Yolanda
Evangelist & Missionary,
Trinidad

I Must Tell This Story

I must tell this story for children every where
I must reach the parents who seem not to care...

Stop look and listen
Can you hear their silent cry?
Stop, look, and listen before they wither and die...

Mark got an "A" in school
Keisha tied her shoe
Brandon learned to spell his name all just for you...

I must tell this story for children everywhere
I must reach the parents who seem not to care...

I didn't get a hug today
You fussed really long
I tried to tell you, Daddy, that I learned a brand new song...

Please don't hit me, Mommy
I won't do it again
I really didn't mean it
God forgive me for my sin...

Stop, look, and listen
Can you hear their silent cry?
Stop, look, and listen before they wither and die...

I must tell this story for children everywhere
I must reach the parents who seem not to care...

Introduction

David, the son of Jesse, called out to the Lord for help from his enemies. The neglect and abuse that was inflicted on him from the man that he had grown to love and respect, King Saul, caused him to run for his life; to seek a hiding place; to trust in the Lord more than ever before.

In the book of Psalms (55:1-8), David cries out to the only one who could save him. Distraught, angry, and fearful, he exclaims, **"Oh, that I had wings like a dove, I would fly away and be at rest!"** He goes on to exclaim how far he would go, the place, and the circumstance of which he must flee from and why. He knows that if God does not rescue him, he will surely die.

Like David, there are so many children crying out for help, rest, and refuge from love ones in whom they trusted for direction, love, loyalty, and security. But, their cries are camouflaged by hostility, bitterness, and depression. Malicious acts, such as neglect, sexual, physical and emotional abuse, and abandonment has crept in to their lives to kill, rob, and destroy them of their innocent youthfulness and joy. Their hearts have been turned to stone. Peering, untrusting eyes hold back the tears that will further expose their vulnerability.

Who can they run to? Where can they hide? What can ease their pain? When will the unjust suffering cease? How can they see God through a world destined to keep them blinded to the truth?

Jesus said, "Suffer the little children, and forbid them not to come unto me: for such is the kingdom of heaven." Matthew 19:14

As parents, guardians, teachers, counselors, coaches, and clergy, we must take our rightful positions in the lives of children. In order to do this, we must consider the following:

First, we must repent for any and all wrongful deeds displayed before them which includes; unconscious, thoughtless, and careless rhetoric spoken before children. We have planted seeds that have taken root in their souls. We have allowed television shows, illicit music, and social media to water those seeds.

Now, as we stand idly by putting the blame on children and youth, as if we had nothing to do with it, we give way to Satan and his demons to give the increase.

Many of our children are suffering due to generational curses that are rooted in our past and present sins of disbelief in God, an unrepenting heart, bitterness, and unforgiveness. God tells us in his word that, "For I the Lord am a jealous God visiting the iniquity of the fathers upon the children unto the third and fourth generation of them that hate me." (Exodus 20:5)

Second, we must surrender our children to God. Hannah was grateful that God blessed her womb with the fruit of His reward. She said, "I prayed for this child, and the Lord has granted me what I asked of Him. So, now I give him to the Lord." And he (Samuel) worshiped the Lord there. We must give our children to God. Shiloh awaits them. God gave His only begotten son that we would have everlasting life. Let us give our children to God so others may see Jesus Christ through them.

Finally, we must express unconditional love towards children. Yes, they will make mistakes. They will show disrespect. They will be ungrateful. They will replicate the very behaviors that characterized us when we were children. Yet, it is still our responsibility to speak love and blessings. If we don't speak life over them, Satan and his demons will speak for us.

'Oh, that I had wings like a dove!" – Touching the life of a child, finds a resting place in the life of children and in the life of parents who desire for God to help them lead and guide their children to Him.

So, "Listen up parents; Listen with an attentive ear. The children want to talk with you without feeling any fear."

God has rewarded us with children. Let us seek His face for their healing and deliverance.

Psalms 55:1-8

Give ear to my prayer, O God: do not hide yourself from my
supplication. Attend to me and answer me:

I am troubled in my complaint.
I am distraught by the noise of the enemy, because of the clamor
of the wicked, for they bring trouble upon me,
and in anger, they cherish enmity against me.

My heart is in anguish within me, the terrors of death have come
upon me, and horror overwhelms me.

And I say,

"Oh, that I had wings like a dove! I would fly away
and be at rest; truly, I would flee far away; I would
lodge in the wilderness; I would hurry to find a shelter
for myself from the raging wind and tempest."

"Wings like a Dove"

The dove is a symbol of peace, new life, and the Holy Spirit. The dove has traditionally been a sign of love and forgiveness.

The most familiar Bible story involving a dove takes place at the baptism of Jesus. All four of the gospels say that when Jesus was baptized in the Jordan River by John the Baptist, the heavens opened and the Holy Spirit descended "like a dove." (Luke 3:22)

The characteristics of a dove can be seen in children. They represent the newness of life. By nature, they are quick to forgive; they are not prideful; their thoughts are pure. But, when we fail to cover them, we rob, kill, and destroy their natural desire for peace, humility, and purity. They become bitter and unforgiving. They find it hard to love and trust. The hurt cause them to want to run away from us – to flee. Their destination is not always one of rest, but one of more hurt and damage. Eventually, their wings are clipped or broken making it hard for them to escape the raging wind and tempest.

The Children's Defense Fund

The Children's Defense Fund has worked very hard for more than 50 years to ensure every child in America has a Healthy Start, a Head Start, a Fair Start, a Safe Start, and a Moral Start in life and successful passage to adulthood with the help of caring families and communities. CDF seeks to provide a strong, effective and independent voice for all the children of America who cannot vote, lobby, or speak for themselves. CDF pay particular attention to the needs of poor and minority children and those with disabilities. CDF encourages preventive investment in children before they get sick, get pregnant, drop out of school, get into trouble, suffer family breakdown, or get funneled into the dangerous Cradle to Prison Pipeline.

Many poor babies in rich America enter the world with multiple strikes already against them and never get on track to successful adulthood. A child is born into poverty every thirty-three seconds, is born without health insurance every thirty-nine seconds, is abused or neglected every forty seconds, is born to a teen mother every sixty seconds, and is killed by guns every three hours.

It is absolutely imperative that we develop and implement comprehensive programs, and policy solutions that keep our children on the road to successful adulthood. This is the only way that we will create a nation and world that is safe, free and filled with the opportunities which too many children now only dream.

Marian Wright Edelman, President/Founder Children's Defense Fund

"The Fruit of the Womb is God's Reward"

Psalms 127:3-5

A Peace That Passes All Understanding

I was sleeping so comfortably. The covers were pulled snugly over my head. I was warm and at peace. All of a sudden! – I felt a tug and then another tug. My eyes popped open! My mind started racing! What was happening?

Something was squeezing my head and pulling my shoulders. I was being abducted, stolen from the warmth and peace I had grown so accustomed to. I was being forced through a long, dark, and wet tunnel. I couldn't breathe! I couldn't hear! I couldn't see! The trauma was too much for me. I thought that I was almost dead until I felt the cold air on my wet body, heard noises all around me, and felt the bright light penetrating my dimly lit pupils. I could barely see anything. After crying out for help, I took a deep breath and fell into an unconscious state, hoping and praying that it was just a dream.

It seemed like months had passed when I finally regained consciousness. As I came to my senses, I focused on a small, thin, brown, moving object. The moving object was wrapping something around my waist while making a strange and funny sound. It was a language that I didn't understand. I was confused and wondered what was going on. Everything in the room was so colorful. I was trying to check it all out, but the small, thin, brown object kept looking at me and making crazy sounds. I figured that I'd better make some crazy sounds, too. I didn't want to appear ungrateful and impolite. I mean, the object had just wrapped something around my waist that felt warm and comfortable. The least I could do was return the favor.

As time went on, I forgot about the warm and peaceful sleep that I was abruptly taken from. I realized that I wasn't dreaming, and perhaps, just perhaps, I was sent to this place to help this strange, small, thin, brown object find the warmth and peace that I had experienced.

After more time had passed, my ability to focus got better. I could now see that this object resembled me – a person. It looked just like me but was just a little bigger and able to do more than me; and, that's only because I was just recuperating from my abduction.

Nevertheless, this person smiled most of the time and was warm, pretty, and very helpful. I started to like this person. We ate together and talked with each other every day. We started to form a bond.

This new place was okay. I didn't have to do anything but lie around and enjoy the scenery. What a life! If I wanted or needed something, all I had to do was talk real loud. Sometimes when I talked real loud for a long time, the person would hug me and walk with me until I finished saying everything I wanted to say. It made me feel as though everything was going to be just fine. I learned to trust this person. I learned to depend on this person. I learned to love this person.

Throughout the darkness, wetness, loud noises, bright lights, and tugging and pulling, this person seemed to have been there the entire time, comforting me and meeting all of my needs and wants. I experienced a peace that passed all understanding.

I think I'll stick around and call her **MOM!**

"Don't Say That"

You get on my nerves

You act just like your father

You are silly and sinful just like your mother

You're so dumb

You can't even stand up straight

Get your fat self over here

Shut up and get out of my face

Who said, "Sticks and stones will break your bones but,
words will never harm you?"

Children Learn What They Live

If a child lives with criticism,
He learns to condemn

If a child lives with hostility
He learns to fight

If a child lives with ridicule
He learns to feel shy

If a child lives with shame
He learns to feel guilty

If a child lives with tolerance
He learns to be patient

If a child lives with encouragement
He learns confidence

If a child lives with praise
He learns to appreciate

If a child lives with fairness
He learns justice

If a child lives with security
He learns to have faith

If a child lives with approval
He learns to like himself

If a child lives with acceptance and friendship
He learns to find love in the world

Author unknown

Dear Lord:

Please speak to me. I have been trying to be a good parent. I have said and done some things to my children that I can't take back. Sometimes I get so angry and frustrated that I wish they were never born. I want to bring them to you, but I do not know how. Sometimes I do not even know how to come to you for myself. I want my children to be more than I am. I want them to know you. I feel as though I have failed at being a parent. I do not want them to suffer for my sins.

Please hear my cry. Speak Lord; I have an ear to hear what your spirit is saying to me!

Love Always,

Mama

Every child's sense of himself is terrifyingly fragile. He is at the mercy of his elders and when he finds himself totally at the mercy of his peers, who know as little about themselves as he; it is because his elders have abandoned him. I'm talking, then, about morale, that sense of self which the child must be invested. No child can do it alone. Children, I submit, cannot be fooled; they can only be betrayed by adults.

James Baldwin, "Dark Days," 1988

If we are good to the child and to other people, he will get from us directly a conception of goodness more profoundly and significant than all the words we may use about goodness as an ideal. If we lose our temper and give to hard, brittle words which we fling around and about, the child learns more profoundly and significantly than all the formal teaching about self control.

Howard Thurman, Disciples of the Spirit, 1963

Daddy, are you picking me up this weekend?

Help Me, Mommy

Seven hundred children and youth filled the church auditorium for a fun filled day of games, singing, dancing, arts and crafts, poetry, drama, and eating, all for the purpose of saying, "No to Drugs and Yes to Jesus."

Everyone seemed to be having such a good time. No one wanted to leave. So many children wanted to perform their rendition of "Just Say No!"

Workshop presenters eagerly and tenderly exposed children to the dangers of drugs. Ministers told stories about Jesus through drama and songs. Some children and adults accepted Christ into their lives.

What a time we had!

As we started cleaning up at the end of the event, I found many items that children had left behind. I was able to return some items that were identified by name, school, or group. Other items remained unclaimed.

There is one item that I still have with me today. It was a letter written by an elementary school student. The letter was tucked away in a small pink and green pocketbook. This is what the letter said:

> Date March 23, 1995
>
> Dear Mommy, I have been beaten up Mommy I haven been like I have Sade rashad forsed me to do sex and I sad no Mommy he just forsed me to do it Mommy I need help
>
> Please write me back

This is exactly how the letter was written. I still have the original copy.

Encouragement

Beyond the dark horizon
Beyond the mass of glum,
If we can see a little hope,
We can see the sun.

If we can mend our broken hearts
Hugging courage from despair,
Then we can grasp a brave new start,
And fight our way to anywhere.

We've suffered from the lack of might,
Yet we have survived the darkest day;
Now all we need is a little light
And, we will find our way.

John Henrik Clarke

"I am Here. I Exist.

And, there's Hope."

Did You Tell Them? Did They Know?

We are numb to the fact that children are dying every day
People are turning their backs on a generation that must lead the way

Is anybody telling them? Do they really know?
Is anybody showing them? Does your Christian light show?

You see, most people want to preach to them, telling them the way
they should go

But, who is willing to walk with them through the rough experiences
as they grow?

A young girl who is pregnant, her mother sucking on crack
A boy packing a weapon, no father to cover his back

A five year old molested, a little girl drinking gin
Roaches crawling everywhere, eviction notice once again

Is anybody listening? Does anybody care?
Come, get your hands dirty
Our children are waiting out there

The harvest is truly plentiful, the laborers are few
Everybody's in the pulpit or sitting pretty in the pew

We are commissioned by God to "go" into a dying and lost world
Snatching our children from the pits of hell
From which they stumbled and fell

The Lord is holding us responsible. He has a special plan for them
We must make sacrifices every day to bring the children closer to Elohim

Exodus 20:5

"For I the Lord your God am a jealous God, punishing children for the iniquity of parents, to the third and fourth generation of those who reject me, but showing steadfast love to the thousandth generation of those who love me and keep my commandments."

If All the Children

If all the children left the world, where would the laughter be?

If all the children left the world, who would look like you and me?

If all the children left the world with wings like a dove; who would give you hugs and kisses, that unconditional love?

Children's Defense Fund

"[We] adults have failed dismally in our most basic responsibility – to protect our society's children from violence."

Marian Wright Edelman (1993)

"I Ain't Trying to Grow Up No Times Soon"

That's right, I'm a kid and I like it like that.
So, you better get used to it.
I'm in no hurry to grow up.
Drink my milk? Eat my vegetables? Please!
Whatever I have to do to get to where you are, I ain't gonna do it.

All you do is complain and fuss and even cuss.
Somebody is always getting on your nerves.
And, you never have any money, always crying broke.
And then you have the nerve to say, "God's gonna make a way."

Yeah, I believe that's true but you sound so religious when you say it.
You know, like when they say, "Praise the Lord" in church and then
talk about people—You know, back biting.

Everything just seems so strange and confusing.
Like the time you told me that Uncle Mike was going to be staying
with us for a while; It was just kind of strange seeing him in your bed
all of the time.
But, I guess that's what family members do.

I remember when I use to sleep with you too.
We just didn't make the kind of noises you and Uncle Mike make.
Anything and everything seem to go in this world.
Whatever happened to all the stuff from Sunday school?
I thought that everybody who went to church was A.O.K. with God.

How come grown ups say one thing and do stuff all together different?
Isn't that called lying? Well, whatever it's called, grown ups seem to
have it down packed.

People singing, "O how I love Jesus", on Sunday and partying and sexing it up on Monday through Saturday seem to be satisfying to you and your friends.

I sure hope I'm still in church like you when I grow up so I can 'have my cake and eat it too'. God's gonna forgive me, right? I can't go to hell; I'm saved, right?

Yeah. That's right. I'm a kid and I like it like that. Too many 'tricks of the trade' being a grown up.

I just don't understand, Dad; you and Uncle Mike? That's Kind of strange. But that's your thing.

I'm out of here cause I ain't trying to grow up no times soon!

Take the Lead?

When fathers are not in their rightful position they allow Satan to have his way with their children. Many of our sons have turned to drugs, crime, and violence due to a large number of fathers not being present in the home or in their children's lives. Many girls have become teen parents and are being physically abused and molested due to absentee fathers. Children are looking for the love and security that God gave to the man to cover them. He possesses the power to conquer the raging beast who descends on his sons and daughters to kill, steal, and destroy them.

Sir, you have given your position away; and, what a mighty position it is. You have allowed the enemy to take future kings and queens and turn them into pimps, whores, drug dealers, drug addicts, and criminals. When the enemy attacks, and he will, who do we have to fight our battles? Who is going to slew Goliath? Who will go into the devil's kingdom and tear down the strongholds that keep our homes, schools, and communities in bondage?

Who will take the lead?

"Postpartum Disgrace"
Through the Eyes of a Child

I see them all the time
I see them everywhere
I see them when I don't want to see them

I try to hide my face
From my race
From the beat down withdrawn
Postpartum Disgrace

I bow my head
Shake my head
Turn my head

Then I count them
Five, ten, fifteen, twenty
Seventy, eighty, ninety, one hundred

On corners, stoops, sidewalks, bars
Passing secret messages through slow riding cars

In the morning, high noon
No light, No life, No vision
No work, no coming home soon

I see them all the time
I see them every where
I see them when I don't want to see them

Brothers, fathers, uncles, sons

Beat down, withdrawn
Black face, my race
Postpartum Disgrace

Ephesians 6:4

" And you fathers do not provoke your children to wrath, but bring them up in the training and admonition of the Lord"

Dear God:

Please help me to be a godly parent. Help me to live a life pleasing to you. Teach me how to plant the seed of righteousness in my children.

Please forgive me for not allowing their father to see them. I've said a lot of nasty things about him in their presence. I no longer want to sow seeds of bitterness.

Please teach me how to pray for my children's father. I know that they need him as much as they need me.

Please help me to put my feelings aside and pay more attention to their needs.

I repent right now and ask for your forgiveness.

In Jesus name, I pray.

Amen

Can We Spend Time Together Every Day, Dad?

Each Day in America

2 mothers die from complications of childbirth

4 children are killed by abuse or neglect

6 children or teens commit suicide

7 children or teens are killed by guns

21 children or teens die from accidents

41 children or teens are injured or killed with a gun

48 children or teens are arrested for violent crimes

65 babies die before their first birthdays

167 children are arrested for violent crimes

384 children are arrested for drug crimes

690 babies are born to teen mothers

874 babies are born at low birth weight

927 public school students are corporally punished

1,151 babies are born into extreme poverty

1,345 babies are born without health insurance

1,903 children are confirmed as abused or neglected

2,315 babies are born into poverty

2,857 high school students drop out

3,617 children are arrested

4,396 babies are born to unmarried mothers

12,816 public school students are suspended

Based on 180 school days a year (The State of America's Children 2014)
http://www.childrensdefense.org/library/each-day-in-america.html

Like Sunday Morning and Going to Church

Sunday morning sure do come fast
Seem like we just got out of church and we right back
Guess I wouldn't mind if folks wasn't so mean
So quiet, I can hear the walls crack

You know, Sister Mary don't like Sister Roe no more
Found out she was gonna be the next preacher in line
And Deacon Brown just look at the floor when pastor preach
He got caught drinking the communion wine

Somebody put a big dent in Aunt Connie's car
She was cursing up a storm right after saying, "Amen."
Said, that jealous whence Sister Mel did it and
God gonna get her for her sin

It's a new man in our church and, he can sing real good
I think Sister Mary likes him
They said, she wore a little dress to church
and bent over right where he stood

Everybody be running to pastor telling him all kind of stuff
They think he's dumb and don't know his call
God be showing him everything
Pastor be seeing it all

But as for me…

It's like Sunday Morning and Going to Church
I just put on my clothes and go sit in the pews
You'll find me right next to the church leaders
That's where I get all my juicy news

"Our Children Must Never Lose Their Zeal for Building a Better World"

Mary McLeod Bethune

I am My Parent's Child

From the time our children are born, they are being molded and shaped in our image. In many instances, they walk like us, talk like us, and act like us. As parents, we shape the world for them.

Socially, emotionally, and psychologically, we teach our children how to respond to their environment. We choose what schools they attend, their religious affiliations, and their extra-curricular activities. We believe that our choices for them will further help shape their world in a positive way. In doing so, I believe that we must consistently evaluate our own lives to make sure that our morals and values lead our children into making healthy and positive choices, as opposed to making unhealthy ones.

Parents can no longer say, "Do as I say and not as I do." If parents are participating in, or practicing risky behaviors in their own personal lives, and acting out their own personal drama before their children, they put them "at- risk" for internalizing anger, stress, low self-esteem, and guilt which can lead to behaviors and conditions such as drug and alcohol abuse, promiscuity, crime and violence, dropping out of school, and eventually, an untimely death.

In essence, as parents, we must return to the better days and ways of interacting with our children. Go back to eating together at the dinner table where conversation is initiated and love for family is paramount. Put down the cell phones and turn off the television and laptops. It's time to hear the heartbeat of this generation.

It is time that we begin to not only focus on urban cultures that, from a media perspective, play out their notorious and uncertain futures on the news, but we must watch and listen intently to all children and youth. Who are these children and youth who wear invisible masks and the proverbial "hoodie" that hide their hostility, bitterness, and depression? Are they poor, middle class, or wealthy? Who is carrying a gun? Who is being bullied? Who is being molested? Who is contemplating suicide or homicide?

As parents, we must consistently evaluate our own lives to make sure that we are not the source of their "CRY."

"Death and Life are in the Power of the Tongue"

Proverbs 18:21

Speak blessings and not curses over children.

What did I do that was so bad and such an ugly thing?

Guilt can damage a child for a life time.

Inside Job

An unforgiving heart I have indeed
For the one who violated me with his seed
To pierce my body, mind, and soul
Someone I trusted, a minister's role

My heart cried out
Why me? Why me?
A father figure I thought you would be

You said everything I wanted to hear
I loved you so
I thought I had nothing to fear

This is my big brother or dad, I would say
As you tickled my body not understanding your play

How disheartened I felt with guilt and shame
Nervously biting my fingers
Was I the blame?

My daddy's locked up and my mama, she's on drugs
You took advantage of my weakness
Pretending to give godly hugs

Slipping in my bedroom
Rubbing on my back
Touching on my private parts
A malicious, sexual attack

You have a deep-seeded problem that little children cannot heal
You got to surrender it to God so your deliverance can be real

Yes. You came upon me like a thief to destroy, kill, and rob
Stalking me day and night to fulfill your inside job

But, God has set my spirit free so I can spread my wings and fly
No longer do I have t endure the pain of a helpless silent cry

I lift my hands and say, "Heavenly Father, help me to forgive what he has done"
He rocks me in his arms and says:
"My sweet child, you have the victory through my Son"

Mistakes

I have a little secret that children are to know
It's about the little mistakes we make as we begin to grow

If you make a mistake
You shouldn't start to cry
Mistakes are not so bad and here is why

Everyone makes mistakes
Oh yes they do
Your brother and your sister
And, your mom and dad too

Big people, Small people
As a matter of fact, all people
Everyone makes mistakes
So, why can't you?

Author Unknown

"Oh, that I had wings like a dove,
I would fly away and be at rest;
Truly, I would flee far away;
I would lodge in the wilderness;
I would hurry to find a shelter for
myself from the raging wind and tempest."

Psalm 55:6-8

Parents,

When you follow wrong inclinations your lives produce evil results, such as, impure thoughts, eagerness for lustful pleasure, idolatry, spiritism, hatred and fighting, jealousy and anger, constant effort to get the best for yourself, complaints and criticisms, the feeling that everyone else is wrong except those in your own little group – and there will be wrong doctrine, envy, murder, drunkenness, wild parties, and all sorts of things.

Let me tell you again as I have before, that anyone living that sort of life will not inherit the Kingdom of God.

Galatians 5:19-21
Life Application Bible

"A child cannot think heaven, know how vast and how merciless is the nature of power, with what unbelievable cruelty people treat each other. He reacts to the fear in his parents' voices because his parents hold the world for him and he has no protection without them."

James Baldwin, 1963

Dear God,

"Please help mommy to stop drinking and smoking that stinky stuff."

I Can Handle It

They said that I was good for nothing
They called me stupid and dumb
They refused to put their arms around me
Squeezing until I was numb

I can handle it

I didn't eat any dinner
And, I stayed home all alone
There's an eviction notice on the door
And no dial tone on the phone

I can handle it

I got kicked out of class again today for
Something that wasn't fair
That old teacher just can't stand me
You know, she really doesn't care

I can handle it

They tried to call my house
To my parent they wanted to speak
I just sat quietly saying to myself,
SMH! She hasn't been home for a week

I can handle it

I'm the man of the house
I've been holding my own for years
I've blocked out all pain and hurt

At nine years old, I shed no tears

I can handle it

Don't worry 'bout me
'Big Mo' got my back
He gave me a gun to cover myself
With the trigger, I'll attack

I can handle it

I'm harder than hard by this crazy life
It's just too much being a little kid
Now, my mom lies in a pool of blood
Something they say I did

I Couldn't Handle It!

David confessed and repented of his sin, but God's judgment was that his child would die.

The consequence of David's sin was irreversible.

When we sin, we set into motion curses that will affect our children, grandchildren, and great grandchildren.

2 Samuel 12:13-18
Life Application Bible – NIV

Time to Reflect

Think back to your childhood. What can you remember about your need for love and affection?

Did you feel that you were loved and respected? Did you receive love and affection through outward demonstrations, such as hugging, kissing, tickling, and holding?

Would you characterize your family as very warm, moderately warm, or cool when it comes to expressing affection?

Parents, it is important to create great and lasting memories for your children. These memories will secure them when the trials and tribulations of life try to overtake them. No matter what your childhood memories were, make a declaration that you will do your best to make their memories better than your own.

Little, Little Children

Lying is my bed last night I said,
God, tell me what to say
Put a poem in my heart that would lead the little children your way

He said, tell them that you love them and show them that you care
Encourage them to follow me and they can go any where

He said, the road through life is not easy
There are bumps and bruises along the way
But, he will get you through it all
If you just take the time to pray

Little, little children when you're loud and wild
God taps me on my shoulder and says,
You use to be a child

Little, little children go ahead and have your fun
Don't be so fast to grow up
Kick a ball, ride a bike, run!

Lying in my bed last night
I said, God tell me what to say
Put a poem in my heart that would lead the little children your way

He said, Give them a hug every day and don't fuss too hard and long
And, remember, they are watching you so make sure your life is no
wrong

So, little, little children, God loves you very much
He put you in this world to give it a very special, special touch

The Cortisol Effect

Severe stress can damage a child's brain. Researchers found that children with post-traumatic stress disorder (PTSD) had high levels of the stress hormone cortisol which were likely to cause a decrease in the size of the hippocampus – a brain structure important in memory processing and emotion.

In the brain, **the hippocampus** is the seat of short and long term memory and also governs spatial orientation (the sense of location which is the ability to move around in an environment).

Humans depend on the hippocampus for learning. The hippocampus is our central organ for learning. Everything we learn, everything we read, everything we understand, and everything we experience count on the hippocampus to function correctly.

The hippocampus is especially vulnerable to ongoing emotional distress, because of the ongoing effects of cortisol.

Cortisol kills hippocamal cells which causes the hippocampus to shrink. When this happens, learning is impaired.

Cortisol stimulates the amygadala which is the fear center of the brain. The larger the amygdala, the more the brain is susceptible to fear.

The **amygdala** is responsible for emotional responses including aggressive behavior. Cortisol stimulates the amygdala while it impairs the hippocampus, forcing our attention onto emotions we feel, while restricting our ability to take in new information.

When cortisol attacks the brain our thoughts fixate on what has triggered the distress, and we become preoccupied with worry, resentfulness, anxiety, anger and sadness. This pushes our brain activity beyond its zones of effectiveness.

As parents, teachers, counselors and coaches, we can lead and guide our children's attention towards more positive experiences causing greater learning as oppose to hostility, bitterness and depression.

Midnight Child

I'm cruising through the city sipping on a Coke
Checking out the people with no vision looking broke…

Sisters looking hungry, butt and breast spill out their clothes
Brothers dissing brothers over a life of crime they chose…

Trash on every corner, drugs filtrate the air
People tossing paper, beer bottles, old mattresses
They don't care…

My vision's getting busy. Can't take it anymore
I'm vexing out quickly. Must escape to higher shore…

As I turn to change directions, small eyes track me down
I slow to catch an image in the midnight of this town…

Standing on cracked marble, front door opened wide
I try to avoid the silent cry of a child on my midnight ride…

Two playing in the alley, one hanging by the bar
A baby barely walking nearly struck down by a car…

Sirens exalt the drama of confusion loud and wild
A bullet pierced the atmosphere killing a midnight child…

With my senses resurrected, I tried to comprehend the mean
I dropped my head and asked the Lord, "Why show me this sorrow-
ful and festering scene?"

He lifted my head gently and placed His hand upon my heart;
"I've placed this burden inside of you for a vision my yoke will impart."

He said, "Reach out and touch the midnight child with gentleness and grace from above."

"I'll deliver them from a life of pain. Through you, I'll show them love."

Hope

Children are very fragile. They find shelter from the storm in our hugs. When we fail to provide that protection, they fail to thrive. We must forever allow them to find comfort and trust in our presence and not our presents. The only way that they can do this is through our love and acceptance of Jesus Christ as our Lord and Savior.

Take this time to accept Him in your heart.

Pray this prayer:

Heavenly Father, I know that I am a sinner.

I believe that you sent your son Jesus Christ to die for my sins.

I believe that He rose from death on the third day that I may have eternal life.

Lord Jesus, please come into my heart right now and save me.

I receive you now as my Lord and Savior.

Amen.

I'm trusting in you, Mommy, to catch me and never let me fall.

I'm trusting in you, Daddy, to be there as I grow big and tall.

Luke 18:15-17

Then they also brought infants to Him that He might touch them; but when the disciples saw it, they rebuked them.

But Jesus called them to Him and said,

"Let the Little children come to me, and do not forbid them; for of such is the Kingdom of God."

"Assuredly, I say to you, whoever does not receive the Kingdom of God as a little child will by no means enter in."

Dear Mommy

I wasn't theirs, but they took me
I hoped for better or worse
I'd been abused, neglected, and rejected
What child could endure such a curse?

They tried to love but in spite of their efforts
I kept getting in the way of loving their own
With all the hugs, family rides and singing, "Sweet Jesus"
My eyes still wept from feeling all alone

What did I do that was so bad and such an ugly thing?
Was it the shortness of my nappy hair or the loudness of my feet?
Was it my messy room and ugly words?
Or, the secret touching that led to my defeat?

You know, I'm having a hard time in school
I've been put out more than one time
I bit the principal and kicked her too
They said I committed a crime

Where are the faces that I once knew and
The places I use to roam?
Where are the hands that once embraced my smile and
The smell and colors of my home?

I'm caught up in this crazy world, "A throw away kid," that's me.

I cry and kick and bite, banging my head on the floor
I have so much anger inside of me,
I just can't take being a kid anymore

I'm screaming to the top of my lungs,
"Mommy, where are you?!"
"I can't do this all by myself
I thought your love for me was true"

It doesn't seem like you're coming back
So, why do I search for your smile?
My heart races to embrace you
It's been such a long while

Mommy, don't you want me?"
Daddy, why can't you be found?
Grandma, stop trying to relive your life
While mine is in constant rebound

I pray that no child ever feels like I feel
Or bear the scars that make me itch
You know, you can't scratch the emotional stuff
It takes time getting out of this ditch

"O, that I had wings like a dove"
I would cover little lonely cries
I would hide them in the shadow of my wings
To shield them from all hurt, anger and lies

Too many "Throw away kids" to count
Lost in a system with no way out
Pushing and shoving to be noticed
Clinging to all hope yet drowning in doubt

But that's okay. I'm gonna make it
That's a promise from my God
No matter what I go through

My heart will never grow hard

So, when you find the time, Mommy,
I'll be waiting always for you
With arms stretched out and a big smile
And Jesus to see us through

Children are the only future of any people. So if the children's lives are squandered and they are not fully developed at whatever cause or sacrifice the people will have cosigned themselves to a certain death."

Francis C. Welsing

Come dance with me
Lift up your wings
The dove is flying
The robin sings

God's children are happy
He's wiped every tear
Joy over flowing
Jesus is here

I Wish I Was Never Born

The silent cries of children permeate the walls of society's institutions every day. The home, the church, and the school are places where our little darlings are suppose to thrive – drinking of life's waters that quench their thirst for love, warmth, happiness, knowledge, and godly instruction. Yet, many adults have failed to honor the great position that has been bestowed upon them – Mother, Father, **– Guardian.**

Webster's Collegiate Dictionary defines guardian as defender; protector; keeper; custodian; or preserver.

The position of guardian, henceforth, calls for adults to be responsible, reliable, and trustworthy to those God gives them charge over.

As guardians over children, adults are assigned a guardian in the form of an angel to watch over them. God gives his angels charge over them to defend, protect, keep, take care of, and to preserve them.

Psalm 91:11 says, "For he shall give his angels charge over thee to keep thee in all thy ways."

Jesus tells his disciples, "See that you do not look down on one of these little ones, for I tell you that their angels in heaven always see the face of my Father in Heaven." Matthew 18:10-14

What if our Guardian Angel failed to honor the great position that God bestowed upon them to watch over mankind? We would constantly fall prey to the enemy. We would not be able to discern danger. Our homes, churches, and schools would be at stake. We would cease to thrive for lack of God's spiritual covering.

Well, that is what is missing in our children's lives. They cannot see, hear, smell, taste, touch, or sense the craftiness of the evil one without our true Guardianship.

In their innocence, they jump, run, play, believe in today and dream of tomorrows. And then, without knowing what hit them, they cry out! –

Why Me?
Such pain and suffering is too much
My heart is heavy
I cannot lift my wings and fly away

I wish was never born
Why did I not die at birth?

Why did I not perish when I came from the womb?
Why was I not hidden like a stillborn child
like infants who never saw light?

My sighing comes before I eat, and my groaning poured out like water
For the thing that I greatly feared has come upon me
And what I dreaded has happened to me

Job 3:1-26

The children cry out like Job. They cannot understand why their faith, hope, and dreams are being shattered unjustly by the hands of their mother, father, guardians.

As mothers, why go through the pain of labor and delivery to bring forth a child and then surrender him to the enemy to be devoured?

National Statistics on Child Abuse

In 2015, an estimated 1,670 children died from abuse and neglect in the United States.

In 2015, Children's Advocacy Centers around the country served more than 311,000 child victims of abuse.

Nearly 700,000 children are abused in the U.S annually. An estimated 683,000 children were victims of abuse and neglect in 2015, the most recent year for which there is national evidence.

About four out of five abusers are the victim's parents.

Two-thirds of children served disclosed sexual abuse (205,438).

Nearly 20% of children served disclosed physical abuse (60,897).

211,831 children received on-site forensic interviewing at a Children's Advocacy Center.

2015 Children's Advocacy Center Raw Statistics (http://www.national-childrensalliance.org/sites/default/files/2015NationalAnnual_0.pdf)

Dying to Know

The healing hands of mommy were far from my touch
As the tears flowed, I prayed and hoped
Don't let this sickness be much

Did it hurt when she got it?
Why did she give it to me?
I was fearfully and wonderfully fashioned for God's longevity

I have so many questions
The thoughts just fill my head
I close my eyes and wonder
Is a coffin like a bed?

Why did they have to tell me?
Did I really need to know?
How can life be here one second and then suddenly cease to grow?

How am I supposed to feel?
Do others have it, too?
Who else knows about it?
Is my secret safe with you?

Can we share a soda?
Can I hug you really tight?
Will my hair fall out and stomach hurt?
Will I lose my friends, my sight?

The medicine is nasty
My nose runs all the time
My breath gets a little short
Some hills are hard to climb

Is God going to fix it?
You know I'm only ten

"God have mercy, please forgive me
I didn't mean to sin"
He whispered in my ear

"My child it's not your fault
The sins of your father revisited you
But your healing I will exalt"

So,

To all my little playmates sick with HIV
It didn't come from God
The devil is the enemy

We'll sing to God and pray
With dove's wings we'll fly
To find rest in Jesus tender arms
For tis not our time to die!

This poem expresses a child's innocent yet desperate cry to God for answers after finding out that she had contracted HIV from her mother at birth. As this ten-year-old child looks to God for the answers, He manifests His grace towards her by gently and tenderly whispering in her ear a message that assures her that His grace is sufficient.

Matthew 19:13-14, states, that when the people brought the little children to Jesus for prayer, the disciples rebuked them. But Jesus told them to leave the children alone and not to get in the way of them coming to Him. God's grace is being manifested through his son Jesus Christ to children who are innocent, weak and possibly sick.

"How can they see God through a world that's destined to keep them blinded to the truth?"

Man, that's My Daughter

Man, that's my daughter that you're trying to get at
That's my little dear one, so, don't you dare say,
"Damn, she's phat!"

Yeah. I saw you looking trying to get a peek.
I saw your tongue hanging out of your mouth
You're so dumb and weak

You can't have any daughters that you protect from ravenous wolves
and thieves
You can't be a young girl's brother or daddy that she cleaves to and
believes

Let her grow up at least until she's twenty-one
Don't put your hands on her virginity
Stop tainting her purity
Stop destroying her youthful fun

Out of all the women in the world you allow your mind to be fixed
on a child a teen… Attacking her in the prime of her life, spinning a
web to destroy a future queen

I know her breasts are rising and her legs are getting thick
Her fingernails are polished… she's filling out so quickly

She wants to be a woman, but it's nowhere near her time
To force her in that direction is a malicious act of crime

Don't touch her innocent beauty for she's a child of heaven's sky
Don't steal her from her mother's nest before she's strong enough to fly

From the rib of a man she was made and from his seed conceived
To be protected and covered as the weaker vessel, by a godly man
who in Jesus believes

But the lust of your flesh held you captive
You would not call out to the Lord
You refused to put on your armor that held your eternal reward

So, you'll go to hell a screaming
Her mind and body God will heal
You were used by the enemy to kill, destroy and steal

But God got the glory
You can't get away with anything
He's her master and her savior
Her true and living king...

Human Trafficking

Human Trafficking is the trade of humans, most commonly for the purpose of sexual slavery, forced labor, or commercial sexual exploitation for the trafficker or others.

Human Trafficking is the third largest international crime industry (behind illegal drugs and arms trafficking). It reportedly generates a profit of $32 billion every year.

Trafficking primarily involves exploitation which comes in many forms including: forcing victims into prostitution, subjecting victims to slavery or involuntary servitude, and compelling victims to commit sex acts for the purpose of creating pornography. Another element of human trafficking is for the removal of body organs for sale.

According to some estimates, approximately eighty percent of trafficking involves sexual exploitation and nineteen percent involves labor exploitation.

According to the United States, 600,000 to 800,000 people are trafficked across international borders every year, of which eighty percent are female and half are children. Some of the most vulnerable individuals for sex trafficking in the United States are runaways, especially LGBTQIA and youth.

It is also estimated that 30,000 people die each year while being trafficked for sex from neglect, abuse, disease or torture.

Help stop Human Trafficking. If you see something, say something.

National Human Trafficking Resource Center Hotline: 1(888) 373-7888

"A child is a cosmos approaching adult chaos"

Jean Toomer, 1931

"A child must learn early to believe that he is somebody worthwhile and that he can do many praiseworthy things. The baby must be made to know that he or she is wanted. The child must have the love of (the family) and protection they give in order to live and flourish."

Benjamin Mays, Best Black Sermons, 1972

"Parents Just Don't Understand"

'Getting To Know Malik'
Who is Malik?

Malik is every black, brown, African male child or youth you will meet. Whether he is a biological or non-biological son; straight or gay; living in the city, suburbs or rural communities; a honor roll student or incarcerated; in a gang or on the church choir; low class, middle class, or upper class, he has a desire to be understood and healed.

He is on the bus stop, at the market, at the mall, or at the corner store. He pops into a place of worship once in a while; he sits in your classroom; he sleeps in your house; he's loud, quiet, funny, shy, withdrawn, outgoing, disrespectful, lazy, handsome, awkward - your son, our sons.

Whoever we believe Malik to be, he is trying to figure out how he fits into the scheme of his home, school, community, and place of worship. He struggles to understand relationships with peers, family members, and authority figures. And, just like most people, he has a desire to be whole in his body, soul and spirit.

The enemy of his soul desires to kill his 'Spirit for Living' before he understands who he is and what his god-given potential is.

The word of God calls Malik, "The Fruit of the Womb – God's Reward."

God calls us (adults) warriors and places Malik in our hands as arrows. It is then our responsibility to direct him in the paths of prosperity in body, soul and spirit.

Therefore, our purpose is to know who we are so that we will be able to help Malik understand who he is. And, as a result, Malik will rise up and be who God called him to be – "The head and not the tail; above and not beneath; rich and not poor; blessed and not cursed."

It is our duty to help our sons get up, stand up, and stay up to be the protectors and leaders in their homes, communities, schools, places of worship, and work. This not only begins the healing process, but it helps to re-establish an almost forgotten and nostalgic way of raising Malik – The Village Approach; The African Proverb that I believe still works: "It Takes a Village to Raise a Child."

Psalms 127:3-5

"Sons are indeed a heritage from the Lord, the fruit of the womb a reward. Like arrows in the hand of a warrior are the sons of one's youth. Happy is the man who has his quiver full of them. He shall not be put to shame when he speaks with the enemies in the gate."

Misunderstood in the Hood

Those little children sure do make me sick!
Get off of my grass!
Little brats
Just don't have no home training
I should call the police
Hey Jimmy! Get my gun
I know how to scare the crap out of them little suckers
Hey! Get off of my car!
Hurry up Jimmy! Give me the gun!
Look at them run. I'll teach them to mess with me
They'll think twice before coming around here again
Bang! Bang!
Ah man! I think I shot one of them
Oh my God! Oh my God!
What happened to my son?
Why did you have to shoot him? He was just playing!
Those little children sure do make me sick!

Beads, Braids and Barbie Dolls

Once upon a time there was a little girl who I invited to a Barbie Doll party. She looked at me like I was crazy and said, "I don't play with Barbie Dolls anymore!" I said, "What! You don't play Barbie Dolls no more?" She said, "No!" I asked her how old are she was. She said, "I'm eight years old..."

After hearing her response, I thought to myself, what happened to make this eight-year-old little girl think that my invitation to a Barbie Doll party was not only crazy but offensive? Had she grown up so fast leaving the innocence of playing with dolls in pre-school, or had the age of technology swallowed her up?

Has technology completely stripped and robbed our daughters of the innocence, novelty, and not to mention, social and emotional growth that can be nurtured through playing with dolls? Have we inadvertently traded our children's childhood for the fast and furious lime light of computer technology causing them to grow up too fast in a world that sells them to the highest bidder?

I can remember my first Barbie Doll. My sisters and I would play with them for hours. Of course that was before cable television and the World Wide Web. We looked forward to a new Barbie Doll every Christmas. What fun!

I also remember when I stopped playing with Barbie Dolls. I was eleven years old. It was the summer of 1971. I was sitting outside on the steps of an apartment building in the Gilmore Homes Projects in Baltimore City. Ms. Lucille was a mean old lady who lived in one of the apartments. She didn't come out much. But, when Ms. Lucille did come out, she wasn't friendly to kids. One day one of my friends and I were playing on the apartment steps because it was the spot with the most shade.

We were having fun dressing up our Barbie Dolls when Ms. Lucille opened the apartment door and said, "Get away from my steps!" Then she looked right at me and said, "You're too big to be playing with dolls anyway!" It was that day that I traded my dolls for boys. By the time I was fourteen years old, I was pregnant.

Before that summer day in 1971, I had no interest in boys. Although my sisters were well into hanging around them, I still liked playing with Barbie Dolls. I didn't know how deeply entrenched her words were. Some adult stole my childhood away – the child within me was stifled that day. The child within me died at the harsh words of an adult.

For years, I tried to find that child who was lost. My search led me down roads infested with drugs, alcohol, domestic abuse, un-forgive-ness, and insecurities. In coming to know Jesus Christ, I found myself in Him. The child within me was resurrected and healed through my call and mission to work with children and youth. Jesus Christ gave me the power and authority to cast down the evil spell that was spoken over me. This put me in position to wage war on Satan and his imps for children and youth so that they too could live a life of happiness and peace in Him.

Listen up parents, teachers, counselors, coaches, clergy, and all adults: Our words have power. Please watch what you say to children and what you expose them to. Let them stay little girls as long as possible. Play with dolls with them. Make beaded jewelry with them. And braid their hair in styles appropriate for their age. Grown up styles will attract rav-enous wolves that strip them of their innocence.

Let no one despise and disrespect your daughter's youth. Teach her how to earn respect by setting an example for her in life, love, faith, and pu-rity. Teach her how to live so others can see Christ in her.

Stifling the Child Within

According to Charles L. Whitfield, M.D., 1987, parents, other authority figures and institutions – such as education, organized religion, politics, the media, and even the helping professions – stifle or deny our Child Within.

In his book, <u>The Child Within,</u> Whitfield refers to that part of each of us which is ultimately alive, energetic, creative and fulfilled; it is our Real Self – who we truly are.

Whitfield contends that, children who grow up in troubled homes often operate in the "lower self." Their experiences of love are neediness, 'chemistry' or infatuation, possession, strong admiration, or even worship – in short, traditional romantic love. He states that, this will and has caused a stifling of their 'Child Within.' And, as a result, they can become stuck at these levels or ways of experiencing love.

In contending with Whitfield, I believe that there are other factors and conditions which cause our children and youth to miss those innocent years of play.

Some of the factors and conditions in the 21st century that stifle the child within are illicit rap lyrics, music videos, violent video games, social media, pornography, poverty, alcohol, tobacco and other drugs, child abuse and neglect, inadequate parenting skills, and post traumatic stress disorder, to mention a few, has caused children and youth to desire a space and place in society that they are not prepared for in their body, soul or spirit.

The above factors and conditions are robbing, killing, and destroying the essence of a child's innocence which can cause emotional and mental illness and disorders. When children are not allowed to fulfill their sea-son of positive childhood experiences, the child within is stifled and eventually dies. This can lead to distrust, aggression, crime and violence, substance abuse, and fear. And, as a result, they fail to prosper in life.

As adults, we must allow children to experience childhood as long as they can. There is nothing wrong with being energetic, creative, and fulfilled. Guard them from the world and Satan. Let them be innocent. Let them play.

They will have enough time to be grown ups. Help them to treasure their innocence now. Tomorrow is coming. Don't rush it. This is the time for children to grow and unfold, not to be bruised before they reach full bloom – 'Their Metamorphosis'.

Once Upon a Time

Once upon a time there was a girl...

She said that she was mad when she got her period because she knew it was time for her to grow up and she was having fun being a little kid.

Once upon a time there was a girl ...

She would cut the hair of her vagina off every time it grew because she thought something was wrong with her. Her mother never talked to her about puberty.

Once upon a time there was a girl ...

She wrote a letter to her mother. It read: "Dear Mommy, I have been beaten up, Mommy. Rashaud forced me to do sex and I said no, Mommy…. He just forced me to do it. Mommy, I need help. Please write back. She was nine years old.

Once upon a time there was a girl ...

She was in the third grade. During lunch time she never ate her food. I asked her why she never ate her lunch. She said that she was on a diet. I asked, why? She said that her mother called her "Fat Ass." She was eight years old.

Once upon a time there was a girl ...

She was four years old with thick and wavy, golden brown hair that complimented her golden brown skin. She wore a big smile every day. One day when she came to school she was not wearing her big smile. When she took off her hat, her thick and wavy, golden brown hair was almost gone. I asked,what happened to your hair? She said, "My mommy's friend cut it off because I wouldn't sit still while she was combing my hair."

My precious daughters, you are a designer's original. There is no one else like you. Learn to love yourself as Christ loves you.

Adverse Childhood Experiences (ACEs)

ACEs are serious childhood traumas that result in toxic stress that can harm a child's brain. This toxic stress may prevent a child from learning, from playing in a healthy way with other children, and can result in long-term health problems.

Frequent or prolonged exposure to ACEs can create toxic stress which can damage the developing brain of a child and affect overall health.

Adverse Childhood Experiences can include:
- Emotional Abuse
- Physical Abuse · Sexual Abuse
- Emotional Neglect · Physical Neglect
- Mother treated violently
- Household substance abuse · Household mental illness
- Parental separation or divorce
- Incarcerated household member
- Bullying (by another child or adult)
- Witnessing violence outside the home
- Witness a brother or sister being abused
- Racism, sexism, or any other form of discrimination · Being homeless
- Natural disaster and war

Exposure to childhood ACES can increase the risk of:
- Adolescent pregnancy
- Alcoholism
- Depression
- Illicit drug use
- Heart disease
- Liver disease
- Multiple sexual partners

- Intimate partner violence
- Sexually transmitted diseases
- Smoking
- Suicide attempts
- Unintended pregnancies

Submitted by the Community & Family Services Division at Spokane (WA) Regiional Health District in Washington State

"We will die without our young people"

Alex Haley

I Am

I am White
I am Black
I am Asian
I am Hispanic
I am Native American
I am Christian
I am Jew
I am Muslim
I am Rich
I am Poor
I am Weak
I am Strong
I am Love
I am Hope
I am the Fruit of the Womb
I am Child
Abuse and neglect has no respect of person

Matthew 18:1-6

At that time the disciples came to Jesus, saying, "Who then is the greatest in the Kingdom of Heaven?"

Then Jesus called a little child to Him, set him in the midst of them, and said, "Assuredly, I say to you, unless you are converted and become as little children, you will by no means enter the Kingdom of Heaven."

"Therefore, whoever humbles himself as a little child is the greatest in the Kingdom of Heaven. Whoever receives one little child like this in my name receives me."

"Whoever cause one of these little ones who believe in me to sin, it would be better for him if a millstone were hung around his neck, and he were drowned in the depth of the sea."

The Evolution of Child Abuse and Neglect

What we consider child abuse and neglect (violence against children) has always existed. In ancient times and well into the Middle Ages, infanticide (the willful killing of a child) was not uncommon, particularly for weak or "deformed" infants and for female children. Children were viewed as the property of the head of the family (the father or senior male householder), and he literally had the power of life and death over them. Abandonments, beatings, whippings, and other forms of physical discipline were common practice. Children had no rights.

In the city of New York in 1874, the case of "Mary Ellen" triggered public concern about abused and neglected children. Mary Ellen was an illegitimate child who had been "indentured" at the age of eighteen months to the care of foster parents. From a neighbor, a mission worker learned that Mary Ellen was being beaten and locked in a room. Later evidence indicated that Mary Ellen had been severely abused and neglected. The mission worker was unable to obtain help for Mary Ellen. The police would not intervene because there was no evidence of the crime; social services would not intervene because they did not have custody of the child; the general attitude was it was wrong to interfere between a parent and a child. Contact was finally made with Henry Bergh, the founder of the Society for the Prevention of Cruelty to animals. Bergh was able to bring the matter into court on the grounds that a child should have the protection that already existed legally for animals. Mary Ellen's case was fully-covered in the newspaper and aroused public concern. As a direct result, the first Society for the Prevention of Cruelty to Children was organized.

Wikipedia, the free encyclopedia

It's the Law

Reporting Child Abuse and Neglect

In Maryland, the child abuse and neglect law requires that anyone who suspects a child has been or is being mistreated must report the matter to the Department of Social Services. In case of child abuse, a report may be made to social services or the police. Any professional who knowingly fails to make a required report of child abuse may be subjected to certain professional sanctions. The professionals identified in Maryland Law include: health practitioners, police officers, educators, and social workers. And, any person who, in good faith, makes a report of abuse or neglect is immune from civil liability or criminal penalty.

Child Abuse is defined as the physical and mental injury of a child by any parent or other person who has permanent or temporary care or custody or responsibility for supervision of a child, or by any household or family member under circumstances that indicate the child's health or welfare is harmed or at substantial risk of being harmed; or sexual abuse of a child whether physical injuries are sustained or not.

Sexual Abuse means any act that involves sexual molestation or exploitation of a child, and includes: fondling, incest, rape, or sexual offense in any degree, sodomy, and unnatural or perverted practices.

Child Neglect is defined as the failure to give proper care and attention to a child including the leaving of a child unattended, under circumstances that indicate that the child's health or welfare is harmed or placed at substantial risk or harm. Child neglect also includes mental injury of a child.

Maryland Department of Human Resources, 2017

Hats Off to Grandparents

I want to dedicate the last poem of my book entitled, 'Generations', to grandparents who are raising grandchildren.

In the last thirty years, there has been a significant increase in the number of grandparent-headed families. According to the American Association for Marriage and Family Therapy (AAMFT), there are approximately 2.4 million grandparents raising 4.5 million children in the United States. Custodial grandparenting occurs when a grandparent assumes responsibility for a grandchild because the grandchild's parents cannot or choose not to care of the child. Some common reasons for custodial grand parenting include parental substance abuse, abuse and neglect, incarceration, HIV/AIDS, mental or physical illness, teenage pregnancy, abandonment, divorce, and death. Although grandparent-headed families are extremely diverse, they are more likely to be African-American, female–headed, and living in poverty.

The American Association for Marriage and Family Therapy research shows that children being raised by grandparents often display developmental delays, depression, anxiety, ADHD, health, physical, behavioral and emotional problems, learning disabilities, poor school performance, aggression, anger, rejection, guilt, and stress.

Becoming a caregiver for a grandchild impacts all aspects of a person's life, emotionally, physically, and financially which can cause grandparents to feel anger at their grandchildren's parents, guilt about their parenting, or embarrassment about their family situation. If or when these feelings arise, grandparents should not talk negatively about grandchildren's parents in front of them which can cause more damage. And, they should allow grandchildren to share their feelings about their family situation.

Hats off to you Grandma and Grandpa! You do a lot for your grandchildren. Please take care of yourself. Join a support group; take advantage of respite services; stay in contact with friends or a faith community; get regular physicals, eat right, and get plenty of rest. You are valuable to your grandchildren even if they are too angry to say so. This poem "Generations" was written just for you.

Generations

I want to know Grandma and Grandpa, too
Tell me all your stories
I want to live as long as you…
What mountains did you have to climb?
What giants did you fight?
Do you have any war scars?
Did you sleep in caves at night?

Were you a slave from Africa?
Did you set the captives free?
Did you march with great leaders?
Did you sail the untamed sea?
How did you get to be so old?
Where do your secrets lie?
Will I someday look like you?
Will my childhood days fly by?
I want to know you, Grandma and Grandpa, too
Tell me all your stories
I want to live as long as you…

"The Family That Prays Together, Stays Together"

In order for our children to succeed in life parents must be in a committed relationship with Jesus Christ. This relationship will lead parents to pray for their children and with their children.

In 1947, Father Patrick Peyton (1909-1992), a Roman Catholic Priest made use of the quote "The Family that Prays Together Stays Together." This quote was used by Father Peyton as the slogan to launch his post World-War II Family Rosary Crusade for the purpose of binding families together through prayer. Other religious orders and secular entities adopted the quote for one reason or another manipulating its wording to meet their particular needs. Nevertheless, this quote has validity:

Mother Teresa, Roman Catholic Nun, international missionary and humanitarian, 1910-1997, prayed: "Be sure to teach the families to pray all together – father, mother, and children. For 'the family that prays together stays together' and if they stay together they will love one another as Jesus loves each one of them... I will be praying that the Lord will bring peace into the world through the love of fathers for their families."

The Christian family is the first place of education in prayer. Based on the sacrament of marriage, the family is the "domestic church" where God's children of all ages learn to pray "as the church" and to persevere in prayer. Nothing happens "on earth as it is in heaven" without the effectual, fervent prayer of the righteous (James 5:16). Prayer is our communication with God. It brings us in close relationship with Him. Several things happen when families pray together: (1) Unity is created (2) God is being glorified and recognized (3) Family members bond together, and (4) A spiritual covering is manifested.

Today, often both parents work due to economic necessity. Unemployment and the high percentage of divorce is having a serious impact on families. More than any time in the history of mankind family leadership must take a more formidable stand on the word of God for the sanctity of family. The breakdown of traditional biblical family values has created avenues/portals for Satan's entrance into homes. The word of God says that "the enemy comes to kill, steal and destroy." John 10:10 (KJV)

The book of James 5:16 states, "The effectual fervent prayer of a righteous man availeth much." Effectual fervent prayer produces positive results within the family which keeps them together through life's struggles and difficulties. Be determined to pray with your family daily.

In conclusion, we cannot continue to hand our children over to alternatives offered by the media. If we spend many hours watching television, surfing the internet, on Facebook or texting, we allow our family values to be conformed by the world's advice and tactics.

Romans 12:1-2 states, "I beseech you therefore, brethren, by the mercies of God, that ye present your bodies a living sacrifice, holy, acceptable unto God, which is your reasonable service. And, be not conformed to this world: but be ye transformed by the renewing of your mind that ye may prove what is that good, and acceptable, and perfect will of God."(KJV)

God has a good, and acceptable, and perfect will for children and families when they stay in the His presence through prayer. Jesus Christ is the "King of Kings and the Lord of Lords. We must always govern our children and families according to His will.

In order to help our children be set free from emotional, mental, and spiritual trauma, Christian principles of the family praying together must be paramount in the home. I admonish all families who profess Jesus Christ as their Savior to immediately begin family prayer. Families must come together in the name of Jesus Christ, in His presence, for His glory, to praise Him, thank Him, adore Him, and ask Him to unite them in His love.

"The Family that Prays Together Stays Together."

"The Grace of the Lord Jesus Christ, and the love of God, and the communion of the Holy Ghost, be with you all."

A Call to Repent
Forgiveness and Restoration

Seeking forgiveness and restoration gives parents spiritual power to pray on behalf of their children.

Repent and confess to God

The Bible says, "If we confess our sins, He is faithful and just to forgive us our sins, and to cleanse us from all unrighteousness." 1John 1:9 (KJV)

Confess means to agree with God… I lied, I was unkind, and I lost my temper. Right now be specific with God…. Silently confess your sins to Him.

Determine to forsake known sin

The Bible says, "He that covereth his sins shall not prosper; but whosoever confesseth and forsakedth his sin shall have mercy." Proverbs 28:13 (KJV)

Make right any wrongs

It is important not only to confess and forsake sin, but also to make things right with those whom we may have wronged.

The Bible says, "And herein do I exercise myself, to have always a conscience void of offence toward God and toward men." Acts 24:16 (KJV)

Renewed fellowship will be the result

The Bible says, "But if we walk in the light, as He is in the light, we have fellowship with one another, and the Blood of Jesus, his son, purifies us from all sin." 1John 1:7 (NIV)

"Oh, that I had wings like a dove!
I would fly away and be at rest;
I would flee away; I would lodge in the
wilderness; I would hurry to find a
shelter for myself from the raging
wind and tempest."

Psalms 55:6-8